CAT CARE

by Hugh Felix

Introduction

Cats make delightful, entertaining and rewarding pets. Although they are much more independent than dogs, they still need to be looked after properly. This includes making sure that they get the right food, are healthy, well groomed and exercised.

This book tells you how to look after your cat. There are sections on choosing a healthy kitten, whether pedigree or not, and making sure that it stays healthy. There's advice on housetraining, feeding, grooming, spaying and neutering, and general health care. At the back of the book there is a useful chart to fill in, to keep all the details about your cat to hand. All in all, this is a book no cat lover should be without.

Do you really want a cat?

The RSPCA estimate that there are something between one million and two million stray cats in Britain today. Many of these animals were once household pets whose owners tired of them and left them to fend for themselves. Before acquiring a cat you must consider carefully whether you really want one, and whether you will be able to look after if properly.

Most people acquire a cat as a kitten. Kittens are great fun, playful, appealing and entertaining. However, after nine months or so a kitten becomes a cat—and it is your responsibility as a cat for the next ten or twelve years. Many stray cats were once the pets of people who wanted a kitten, but abandoned it once it grew into a cat. To do this is cruel and irresponsible. You must ask yourself when looking at a fluffy little kitten whether you will still want it when it is a full grown cat—if the answer is no, do not acquire the kitten.

Assuming that you do like cats, and want to own one, you must consider whether you can offer it a suitable home. Although cats are not as demanding as dogs they have certain needs that must be filled if they are to be happy.

They must have the opportunity for exercise. Take a look at where you live—how is the cat going to get in and out, can you provide a cat flap, or will you be around to let it in and out? If you live in a flat you must look at this question particularly

CATS ARE CREATURES OF HABIT

carefully—generally speaking a high rise flat will not make a good home for a cat.

Cats also need the company of other cats, usually they can find this quite easily if they are free to come and go as they please. If their movements are likely to be slightly restricted, or if you live somewhere where there are few other cats, then it may be better to get two cats to provide company for each other.

You must also make sure that you have the time to take care of your cat properly. This means first of all that you must have time for regular feedings. Cats are creatures of habit, and will become very unhappy if their meal times keep changing because you are too busy to establish a routine.

Secondly, and perhaps most importantly you must have time to spend with your cat, not just talking to it and petting it occasionally, but also being around the house. Cats need human company—if they don't get it they become bored and unhappy. If you are likely to be out all day and half the night, don't get a cat—you haven't enough time to spend with it.

You should also consider how much money owning a cat will cost you. Besides the food there are also vet's bills to be paid, and boarding fees when you go away on holiday. All of these add up.

Finally two golden rules. Never buy a cat (or any other animal) as a present for someone unless you are absolutely certain that the animal is wanted—if in doubt don't do it. Secondly don't buy a cat for a child to look after 'to make them responsible'. It never works. Unless the child is already very responsible, you will end up having to look after the cat. The unfortunate animal will end up unwanted and unloved through no fault of its own.

Pedigree or not?

Most pet cats are mongrels; the product of two or more different breeds. Being a mongrel doesn't carry the same stigma with cats as it does with dogs. A mongrel cat can be just as attractive as a pedigree. In fact it may also have a number of advantages over a pedigree.

Firstly they cost considerably less than a pedigree animal; in many cases they may even be free. Of course they cost the same amount to keep and feed. Secondly, they are often stronger and healthier than pedigree cats. In some cases pedigree cats can also be rather highly-strung, and so less good with small children.

Another, often overlooked advantage of a mongrel cat is that there is no need to worry about the animal being stolen. With a valuable pedigree animal this may be a very real worry.

Most people getting a pedigree cat will have kept a cat before, and know exactly what they are now looking for in a pedigree.

One of the advantages of a pedigree, often overlooked by the first time owner, is that knowing the breed, it is possible to predict the cat's personality. With a mongrel cat acquired as a kitten, this is not possible. The fixed personality of the pedigree can also be a disadvantage; if you don't take care you may acquire a breed for its looks then find its character is quite unsuitable for the way you live.

There is also a tendency to mollycoddle a pedigree—this can lead to overfeeding which may in turn make the cat ill. In general a pedigree cat will need more looking after than a mongrel, particularly if the cat is a long-hair. This need not be a problem—many people may welcome the extra involvement.

Also on the positive side acquiring a pedigree cat may be the first step in a lifelong interest in the breed, involving showing, and even breeding for yourself.

Cat types

Cat types are rather difficult to grasp at first—the system of classification is much more complicated than with dogs, and the different breeds are closer to each other.

Colour

Each breed of cat will be available in various different colours. Therefore most breeds are known by both a name and a colour—for example, white Angora. Black is the most common colour, other colours include white, cream, red (ginger), blue and brown.

TABBY CAT

The cat may be one single colour throughout—known as a *self* colour, or it may have a coat made up from a combination of colours.

The most common combination of colours is that found on the *tabby*. Here the coat consists of dark stripes or spots on a light background. There are four officially recognised tabby patterns—classic, spotted, ticked, and mackerel.

TORTOISESHELL

SIAMESE

When the two colours are quite distinct (rather than one being a darker version of the other) then the coat is called tortoise-shell. Breeders sometimes also refer to them as *torties*. Often the coat also contains patches of white, and is known as tortie and white.

A cat that has a pale coat may have dark 'points'—that is, the feet, end of the tail, ears, and face are dark. The Siamese cat is one example of a cat that shows this patterning.

MANX

Short haired cats

Short haired cats are divided into two
groups—British short hairs (also known as
European), and foreign short hairs.

British short hairs have compact bodies,
fairly flat faces, and broad heads. Most of
the individual breeds have their own distinct
colours. Varieties include the Scottish Fold,
so called because of the way its ears are
folded down, and the Manx cat—with its
very short tail.

The Siamese is probably the most well known of the foreign short hairs. Foreign short hairs in general have shorter fur than their European equivalents. Their bodies are much more elongated, and their faces are sharp, with a narrow head and long errect ears. Their tails are long and pointed.

Other foreign short hairs (also refered to as 'Orientals') include the Russian Blue, Abbysinian, Burmese, Foreign white and the various Rexes.

ABBYSINIAN

Long haired cats

The most common type of long haired cat is now the Persian. It has quite short legs, a round face, and a thick body. The coat is heavy, particularly on the tail, and in the ruff around the neck. Varieties of Persian cat include various self colours, tabbies, and tipped colours (the Chinchilla for example).

PERSIAN

ANGORA

Angora cats were the original long haired cats, the name deriving from Ankara in Turkey. They have now been overtaken in popularity by the Persians. Their shape is much more distinct and cat-like than Persians. Although the coat is long, it is not as fluffy as in the Persian—it's usually described as silky The head is wedge shaped and the ears erect.

The latest development in breeding is to produce a long haired cat that has some of the characteristics of the oriental short hair--examples include the Himalayan, Birman, and Balinese.

Where to get your cat

If you are buying a pedigree cat you will want to get it from a specialised breeder. Breed clubs and fancy organisations will be able to provide a list of breeders. Otherwise breeders often advertise in specialist magazines. Sometimes kittens are sold at cat shows.

When buying a non-pedigree cat it is best to avoid buying from a pet shop if possible. The kitten will have to suffer the double disturbance of leaving its mother and going to the shop, then going from the shop to you. This may make it slow to settle. In addition it will not have been handled as much as a cat coming from someone's home, and this will make it less tame— important if you have young children.

The other risk when buying from a shop is of illness; infection can spread very quickly in a pet shop. Make sure that you get certificates of vaccination against enteritis and flu. A written guarantee of good health is a sign of good faith, but it doesn't protect against the heartbreak of having a kitten fall ill and die.

The best place to get a kitten is from a family home—preferably with young children. This means that you can take a look at the mother as well as the kittens, and probably get the pick of a litter. If there are children in the house the kittens will probably have been handled quite a lot. This helps to make them tame, and is especially important if you have young children.

The best time of year to acquire a kitten is in the spring, there are more kittens looking for good homes at this time, and so you will have a better choice. Vets often have a list of kittens looking for homes. Otherwise newsagents' notice boards are a good source, as is the local paper. If you have children they may well hear of kittens available at school.

Don't accept a kitten that is less than eight weeks old—they are too young to leave their mother before this age. Ideally the kitten should have been weaned onto solid food and wormed before you take it—do ask about the worming, if it hasn't been done you must do it yourself (see page 55).

The Healthy Cat—
what to look for

When choosing your cat remember that over the next ten to fourteen years you will be investing a considerable amount of time, money, and most importantly, affection in it. Time spent in making sure that a kitten or cat is healthy to start with will avoid unhappiness later on. Although many faults may be put right by a vet the money involved may be considerable, and the animal may still not be really healthy afterwards.

The first thing to look for when choosing a cat or kitten is a lively responsive personality. When choosing from a litter of kittens look for one that is active and playful, and responds well to handling. Personality is more difficult to judge in an adult cat, but don't accept a cat that seems unfriendly or slothful.

Next examine the coat; it should be unmatted and glossy. Does the cat scratch itself frequently? If it does look for the reddish areas on the skin that indicate it has fleas. Look also for bald patches that may be caused by ringworm, and any other skin sores.

Check the ears for waxy or other secretions that may be caused by an infection. If there is a dark brown dry wax in the ears this means that there are mites; if you want to take the kitten, these mites can be dealt with quite easily by a vet.

The nose and eyes should also be checked for any secretion or discharge; they should both be clean. Eyes should be bright, and the nose cold and slightly damp. A white cat that has blue eyes may be deaf from birth. Check for a response to loud noise.

Hold the mouth open and look inside; a healthy cat will have pale pink gums. Check for any redness in the mouth and throat that may mean there is an infection. In a kitten the teeth should be clean and white.

A kitten should be fairly plump, but if the stomach protrudes this may indicate the presence of worms. If there is a lump the cause may be an umbilical hernia.

Don't accept any cat that has diarrhoea: the signs are a sore and dirty anus or a wet tail. In a female the vulva should be clean and free of any discharge.

Watch the kitten or a cat as it walks, are the legs straight? Is the tail kinked? Does it stumble, or limp? Count the toes, there should be four on each foot, as well as the dewclaw (the thumb) higher up on the inside of the front legs. Kittens are quite often born with extra toes. One extra toe per foot may be a bit of nuisance if it grows too long: don't accept a kitten with two or more extra per foot. Remember that a cat can't be shown if it has extra toes—in a pedigree this may be a reason for getting the price down.

Finally check the sex: it is by no means uncommon for kittens to be sexed wrongly. Hold the kitten up so that it faces away from you, and lift the tail. With both sexes you will see two openings. In the male (see below) the two will be about half an inch apart, with the scrotum in between them, although at this stage all you will see is a sightly raised area. In the female the vulva is very close to the anus, and is a vertical slit, rather than a hole, as in the male (see below).

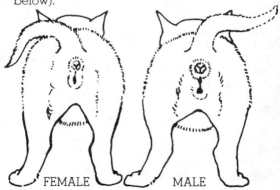

FEMALE   MALE

Acquiring an adult cat

In most cases you will acquire an adult cat involuntarily. One day the cat may simply walk into your home and decide to stay. This often happens when a family move, and leave the cat behind. The cat adopts you as its new family. Obviously if the cat has a name tag you should check to see whether the owners wish to reclaim their cat. Otherwise the cat is yours if you want to keep it.

In other cases you may get an adult directly from friends who are moving abroad, or who, for one reason or another, no longer want a cat.

The first thing to do with an adult is to have it checked by a vet to see whether it is healthy, and whether it has been neutered or not.

You may find that the cat has some bad habits—some of these can be changed, but most you will just have to learn to live with.

The advantage of an adult cat is that you can see exactly what you are getting, both in looks and personality. This is particularly useful if you have children—some cats respond well to children others may be quite bad tempered.

Bringing home a kitten

Before you bring your new kitten home, there are a few preparations you should make to ensure that you get off to a good start.

Getting ready

The first thing you will need is some kind of cat carrier to bring it home in. Don't carry it in your arms—it will be under quite a lot of stress, if you carry it yourself there is bound to be some kind of accident.

A CARDBOARD BOX MAKES A GOOD BED

There are various kinds of carrier available. The cheapest is made of cardboard—however this may only be used a few times as it can't be cleaned and isn't very strong. If the journey is long, or you are likely to want to carry the cat about quite often, it is better to get one made of a stronger material—wicker for example.

At home, you will need to have some kind of a bed available—cats are creatures of habit, and if the kitten gets used to sleeping on a particular chair now, it may be difficult to get it to use a bed later on.

If you don't want to buy a bed at this stage you can make one quite simply from a cardboard box. Cut the sides down to a height of six inches (15cm) or so. Now cut a gap out of one of the sides to act as a doorway. The bottom should be covered with newspaper, followed by a piece of old blanket (or similar). A bed made from a cardboard box has the advantage that it can be thrown away if it becomes dirty or chewed.

Whichever kind of bed you get, it should be put in a warm draught-free place, where the kitten won't be disturbed too much.

You should also provide separate bowls for food and water. These are better than saucers or dishes as they are much less likely to spill. They are also easier to keep separate from your own crockery, and so avoid any spread of infection. The bowls should be placed where the kitten will be able to eat without being disturbed.

Before getting any food you should check with the present owner to find out what the kitten is used to—you should start them off on this, even if you switch to something else later on.

Perhaps the most essential thing to have ready is a litter tray—one is the minimum, but in the long run you will want several if housetraining is to go smoothly. The trays can either be filled with peat, or more conveniently, special cat litter. This is sold in pet shops and some supermarkets.

Put one tray close to the bed, and distribute any others at strategic intervals around the living area.

At first the kitten should be restricted to one room. Make sure that you choose a room that is warm, dry, and free from draughts. Avoid a room containing heavy or immovable furniture that the kitten may become stuck behind, or one full of fragile ornaments.

The first day

The best time to collect a kitten is at the weekend. It will need a lot of attention during the first few days, and may be difficult to settle if left on its own too much. Choose a weekend when all the family have plenty of time to devote to the new arrival. Avoid times when there are people other than the immediate family around the house, or when there is a lot of coming and going.

If you have very young children it may be a good idea to choose a time—evening for example—when they will not be about for a few hours. Explain to older children that they must be very gentle to the kitten at first. Although some handling is a good thing, the kitten must be given time to explore and make itself at home.

Before you let the kitten out of its carrier, make sure that all the doors and windows are closed—kittens can move surprisingly quickly.

Let the kitten out and provide something to drink—milk or water depending on what it is used to. Let it wander around on its own at first, then try to draw it into play—a piece of wool makes a good toy. When it has settled you can handle it a little—stroke it rather than picking it up. Show it where its bed is, and allow it to sleep if it wants to.

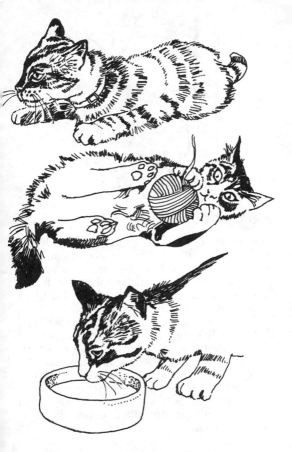

DON'T ENCOURAGE BAD HABITS

After an hour or so it may be ready for some food, but don't worry if it doesn't eat much at first. Get a diet sheet from the previous owner, and stick to this, and to the kitten's regular mealtimes, even if it doesn't seem to want to eat much at first.

After it has eaten put it on the litter tray, if it uses the tray reward it with plenty of praise. Keep the kitten in the one room for the first day. After this you can gradually let it explore other rooms, making sure that it can't get out of doors.

At this stage don't encourage bad habits—don't let the kitten climb the curtains and so on.

Housetraining

As long as you make sure that the kitten spends most of its time in a room containing several litter trays housetraining should not be a problem—its mother will have done most of the work in its previous home. Make sure that you put the kitten on a tray after each meal, and that you praise it when it uses a tray. Empty the tray and provide fresh litter as soon as a tray has been used—the kitten won't use a soiled tray.

ther pets

ther cats or dogs should be kept out of the ay when the kitten first arrives. The kitten ill smell that there is another animal in the ouse and be able to get used to this smell. After a few hours remove the kitten to another room and allow the other pet to sniff around for a while. You can now let the animals make a brief introduction—watching them carefully, particularly if the other animal is a dog. They should then be separated once more.

Introduce the two again gradually over a few days until they are quite used to each other. Don't try to feed them in the same place until they are quite happy together. If they tend to fight at mealtimes then separate them again.

Going out

Let the kitten get thoroughly used to its new surroundings before you let it go outside. Normally you should wait at least four or five days before letting it out.

To start with you should carry it outside and let it walk about for just a few minutes, keeping an eye on it the whole time. Don't let it out at all on very cold days.

After doing this a few times you can let it walk in and out on its own—again keep a close eye on it. When you are sure that it is

capable of finding its way in and out you
can let it out on its own provided you have
a garden away from a busy road. Make sure
that you get a collar and name tag before
you do let it out on its own.

Injections

After the kitten has been with you for two
weeks or so, it will be ready to have its
injections. These protect the kitten against
the two most common cat diseases:

Cat flu: although rarely fatal this can cause a great deal of discomfort, and can be dangerous if the kitten is inclined to be rather weak. If may also leave a permanent problem with breathing or the tear ducts.

Feline enteritis: this is a much more serious disease. It may kill a cat within one day of contracting it. The symptoms are vomiting, and diarrhoea. Kittens are particularly susceptible, and the disease tends to run in epidemics through the local cat population.

You should make sure that your cat has had these protective injections before you let it out of your garden. Make sure that you keep the certificate the vet gives you—many catteries will not board cats without certificates.

Feeding your cat

Unlike humans and dogs, cats are solely carnivores. This means that they can only get the vitamins and minerals they need from meat—we are much more adaptable. For this reason you need to take some care to see that your cat is getting a proper diet—you cannot expect it to survive on scraps and odds and ends.

All this means that cat food has to contain vitamins and minerals that dog food does not. It must also have more first class protein. This often makes cat food more expensive, but don't be tempted to feed your cat on dog food to save money—you may make the cat ill. In fact, feeding cats on dog food is a common cause of blindess.

Canned food

The easiest, safest, and best way to feed your cat is on canned food. It is important to check the label to see what the food is suitable for. Many foods require supplements if fed to kittens or lactating females. Foods described as 'all meat' may also not provide a balanced diet, as may 'gourmet' meals. Again check with the label. Do chop and change flavours and brands though—otherwise the cat may get bored.

Dry food

Dry food has become increasingly popular recently. It is cheaper and less heavy than tinned food and will stay fresh on the plate for long periods. It also provides much better exercise for the jaw, and helps keep the teeth clean. However, there are a number of disadvantages to this kind of food.

The first is that they are often not nutritionally complete, so with kittens and pregnant queens it is important not to give dry food alone. It should be alternated with canned food, and the cat should be offered milk as well.

The most important problem with dried food however is simply the fact that it *is* dry. Cats get much of their liquid intake through their food. Because of this if you are feeding your cat on dry food you must make sure that it drinks plenty of water (or milk).

The cat should drink at least a large cupful of water a day, more in hot weather. This can either be given separately or mixed with the food itself in the form of a gravy.

If the cat doesn't get enough liquid it leads to all kinds of painful, and sometimes dangerous problems with the bladder and urethra. For this reason you should not give dry food to any cat that has had problems in the past with its bladder, or has suffered from cystitis. You should also stop giving dry food to any cat that is not drinking enough water.

Perhaps the best way to give dry food is in alternation with canned food—this gives many of the advantages of dry food, while eliminating the problems.

Fresh food

When feeding fresh food the important thing is to provide variety. Cats are not good at regulating their own intake—for example they will quite happily eat liver every day, even though to do so will make them ill. The cat will need about eight ounces (200g) of meat per day. This can take the form of fish, rabbit, other red meat, offal etc, and all these types should be given in rotation. In addition the cat should be given milk to drink. In some cases it may be a good idea to give a vitamin supplement. Fish should always be cooked.

Fussy eaters

Because of the particular nature of the cats nutritional needs, it is important to give the cat as much variety as you possibly can. If you stick to just one kind of food in one flavour the cat may then refuse to eat anything else, and this can easily cause an imbalance.

To avoid producing a fussy eater you should get the cat used to eating different things from an early age. If you are feeding it mainly on canned food give some dry and some fresh food for a change.

All cats are fussy about the temperature of their food, they like it to be at room temperature or slightly warmer—they often won't eat it straight from the fridge, and won't neccesarily come back to cold food when it has warmed up. Let the food warm up before offering it to them.

If the cat is reluctant to eat, and continues to be so, despite being offered different food, it may indicate there is an illness—take the cat to the vet.

How much?

This will depend on the individual cat. As a rough guide, a cat weighing four pounds (2kg) will need four ounces (120g) of tinned food per day or one ounce (25g) of dry food per day. A cat weighing twice this amount will need twice as much food. A cat that is giving milk will need three times as much food as a cat that is not. A pregnant cat will need about half as much food again as one that is not pregnant.

These figures should only be used as a rough indication. Your main guide should be the cat itself. Provided it is not already either fat or skinny, you should feed the cat enough to keep its weight at its present level—if its weight changes you are feeding it the wrong amount.

When?

Kittens need to be given their food in at least three or four small meals, rather than two large ones. The same is also true of an adult that is pregnant or lactating.

When feeding adults on fresh or canned food it is best to split the day's food into two meals. To avoid flies, give the cat half an hour or so to eat, then remove the food. Remember to keep feeding times regular— if you don't, the cat will soon remind you.

Dry food can be given in one meal, and this can be left out all day for the cat to help itself to. You must make sure water is available all day as well. Cats rarely over-eat on dried food.

Grooming

Short haired cats

Cats are, of course, well known for their cleanliness. Most of the time short haired cats will keep themselves well groomed without their owner's help.

Twice a year, they will moult, and at this time they need to be groomed frequently. If this is not done they will swallow a large amount of fur in the act of grooming themselves. This fur will form into balls in the stomach, and these can cause all kinds of quite serious internal problems. Watch out for signs that the cat is moulting, and groom once a day when it is. Doing this also has the advantage of preventing the furniture from becoming covered with cat hairs.

Cats also swallow a certain amount of hair in the normal process of grooming—this is not a problem, but they sometimes make themselves sick in order to get rid of it. The usual way of doing this is for them to eat grass. Make sure that they can get some grass somewhere.

It is a good idea to groom short haired cats occasionally when they are not moulting. They get used to being combed, and it lets you keep a general check on their skin and fur. You can also remove any burrs that the cat can't get rid of for itself.

Long haired cats

Long haired cats have been especially bred over the centuries as pets. Unlike the short haired cat, there is no equivalent in the wild. The cat's fur is far too long for the cat to be able to look after it itself. Therefore it must be groomed regularly—once a day is normal

This process of grooming is not a luxury, it's absolutely vital to the cat's well being. Not to groom is a cruelty. Before getting a long haired cat you should think carefully about whether you can regularly devote the time needed for grooming.

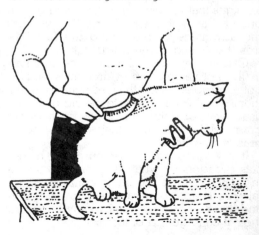

How to groom

A brush may be used on short haired cats that are not moulting. However, you should use a comb on long haired cats, and short haired cats that *are* moulting.

Hold the cat firmly and comb in the direction of the fur, making sure that the comb goes right through the coat. Don't stop even if the cat struggles—just take a firmer hold. Most cats that have been groomed regularly will present no problem, but one that is not used to it may object—if necessary get help in holding the cat.

Washing

In the normal course of events cats don't need washing; they will keep themselves clean. The exception to this rule is an old cat, who may have become lazy about grooming itself, and who will need washing from time to time.

If, however, a cat becomes very dirty for some reason—covered in mud for example—it may stop washing itself. You will then need to bath the cat. This is particularly important when a cat gets covered with a poisonous substance, like creosote, gloss paint, oil, paraffin etc. If the cat is allowed to try to clean itself it will absorb the poison—it must be washed straight away.

Before you start to wash the cat, make sure that it has its collar on—you will need it to hold on to when the cat is wet and slippery. Fill a suitable container or sink with warm (not hot) water. Don't try to put the cat in at this stage: instead hold the collar and pour some warm water over the cat. It will be much more resigned about going into the water once it is already wet.

Washing-up liquid is quite suitable for most occasions. If you have to wash an old cat regularly you may like to use a special shampoo instead. If the cat is covered with an oily substance Swarfega can be used in place of washing-up liquid. Keep water and soap away from the eyes. To prevent struggling use a firm pressure to hold the head slightly downwards.

Make sure that you rinse all the soap off properly, then remove the cat and dry using a towel. Don't let it out of the house for a few hours, and keep it out of draughts.

Eyes and nose

If you live in a house with central heating, your cat's nose may tend to become dry and cracked, particularly in winter. Rub gently each day with baby oil until the nose is better.

The cat's eyes should be clean and bright. If they tend to get gummed up, they can be cleaned using cotton wool dipped in slightly salted water.

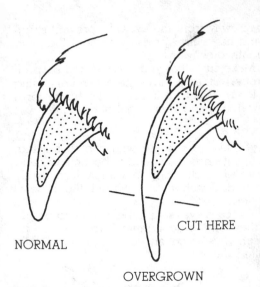

NORMAL

CUT HERE

OVERGROWN

Claws

In most cases the claws will not need attention. However, an old cat, or one that doesn't get a lot of exercise may develop long claws. Use the illustration above to guide you as to whether your cat's claws are too long. You can cut the claw quite easily yourself, using clippers from a pet shop. Cut where shown—don't cut into the quick, which is pink. If in doubt get the vet to show you how to do it.

Spaying and Neutering

Because of the size of the stray cat population in this country the RSPCA recommends the neutering of all pet cats, with the exception of pedigree animals required for breeding. There are many arguments in favour of this procedure.

An intact tom is not suitable as a domestic cat. Generally speaking most of his time will be spent looking for female cats (queens) that are on heat.

Besides keeping him away from home all day, and perhaps for several days on end, this search is almost bound to involve him in a considerable amount of fighting, with consequent injuries. All this wandering makes him more likely to be hit by a car, and the ceaseless activity reduces his life-span.

He will also, when home, mark his territory by spraying pungent urine to establish a domain.

In contrast, the neutered tom makes a very good pet, provided the operation is performed at the right age. He will be more affectionate and tend to stay nearer home. Contrary to popular belief, neutered toms do not become fat and lazy, and they are

47

just as good mousers as entire cats. In fact they are often better.

An entire female will produce up to three litters of three or four cats per year. This number of kittens will be far too many to give away, and inevitably you will have to have many of them destroyed. The demands of this kind of breeding also places a severe strain on the mother. She will be much more inclined towards illness than a spayed female, and will not live as long.

In addition to the above, the entire female has various undesirable characteristics. When in heat she will produce distressing and noisy calls. Also, she is bound to be called upon by local toms, who will fight, and spray and generally make a nuisance of themselves.

In order to be effective in altering the cat's behaviour the operation of spaying or neutering has to be carried out when the cat is still a kitten. Your vet will be able to advise you of the best time. As a rule it is when the cat is about five or six months old. If you leave the operation too late the cat will continue to behave as though it is capable of breeding, even though it is not.

The operation itself is routine, simple and safe. The cat is given a general anaesthetic, and is quite back to normal within a couple of days.

Your cat's health

Seeing the vet

Cat owners often have difficulty deciding whether a cat is ill or not. One of the usual signs is that it will creep away somewhere on its own, and be unwilling to eat its food. In other cases however, the signs may not be so obvious.

If you feel, for whatever reason, that something is wrong with the cat don't be afraid to consult the vet. You needn't take the cat to the vet to do this; ring first, and ask. It may be that the vet will be able to reassure you that there is nothing wrong over the phone.

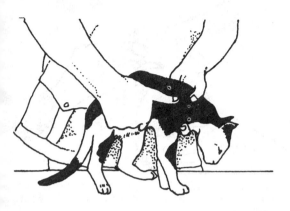

Possible causes for concern include the following:-

Skin and fur: bald patches, persistent itching, sores or inflamation.

Eyes: persistent watering or discharge, eyes frequently bloodshot or cloudy.

Ears: frequent itching or head shaking, build up of wax.

Stomach: bulging unnaturally, over sensitive, persistent vomiting.

Defecation: pain while urinating, persistent diarrhoea or constipation, blood in stools.

Lungs: any kind of breathing difficulty, wheezing or coughing.

Limbs: unexplained or untreatable limps, or any stiffness.

Unless the animal is injured, and needs to be kept still, you should not carry it in your arms, use a basket or box.

The vet may prescribe medicines that you will have to give to the cat. Tablets can be a problem. Cats will often refuse to eat food that has a crushed tablet mixed in with it. The simplest thing is to pop them in the cat's mouth yourself. Although the cat may struggle a little, this is not cruel. Open the cat's mouth with one hand and hold it open, use the other to place the tablet at the back of the cat's tongue. Shut the mouth, and hold it shut for a few seconds to encourage swallowing.

Opening the mouth in the same way will also let you give the cat a liquid medicine. Don't give too much at once, and let the cat swallow before giving more.

Eye drops are given by holding the cat's head up and slightly back. Put the drop in the corner of the eye nearest to the nose, and hold the head still for a few seconds before releasing.

Again, you should hold the head up and slightly back to give ear drops. After giving the drops hold the head still and rub gently just behind the ear to help the liquid to penetrate.

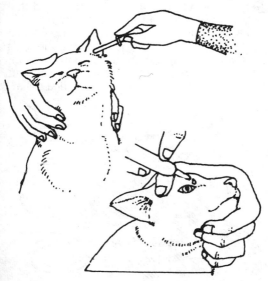

Parasites

Like most animals, cats have certain parasites that will live on them, given a chance. Even the cleanest cat may pick up parasites, but regular grooming and examination will let you deal with the problem at the early stages.

The most common parasites are fleas; the cat scratches frequently, and the skin shows red marks. You may see a flea on the fur—they are small and black. You may find that you or your family are bitten by them.

Treat for fleas using a spray, or powder. It is very important that you also treat the cat's bed and any furniture it regularly sits in, since this is where the eggs will be. You can guard against re-infestation with a flea collar.

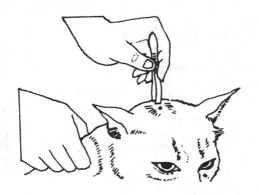

Your cat may also suffer from ticks. You will feel these as lumps on the skin. Don't try to pull them off, as the head will left behind. Instead, cover them with butter (or similar) and leave for about an hour. This will suffocate them, and they can then be pulled off easily.

Cats are prone to having worms. Kittens are wormed as a matter of routine. When acquiring a kitten, find out if this has been done. Roundworms cause diarrhoea, vomiting and loss of appetite. They are simple to treat using tablets. Tapeworms are more tricky—see a vet if you suspect them.

Ear mites are a particular problem with kittens. The signs are frequent scratching and head shaking, and a dark brown wax in the ear—see a vet.

Pregnancy

Pregnancy in cats lasts something between sixty and sixty-five days. However you will probably not realise that the cat is pregnant for a little while. For this reason it is a good idea, if you have an unspayed queen, to make a note of the date each time she is in season (see page 49 for how to tell when this is). When you realise that she is pregnant you can work out the approximate date the kittens are due using the date of the last time she was in season.

A pregnant cat requires little special treatment. Reduce handling to a minimum after the first two weeks. In the last month or so she will require much more food than usual; let her eat as much as she wants (see page 39). Make sure she is getting a proper diet—avoid dry foods. Vitamin tablets may be necessary, consult the vet.

As the end of the pregnancy draws near provide a place for the kittens to be born. The best thing is a medium sized cardboard box. Cut a hole in one of the sides as a doorway, and line the inside with old newspapers (these are better for the job than cloth). The top of the box should have a removable cover. Put the box in a warm, dry, quiet place, and don't disturb the mother when she goes into the box—she

must feel safe in there.

Normally the birth will occur without any help being needed. The mother will clean up the kittens afterwards and deal with the umbilical cords. If she seems to be having difficulty or straining, and this goes on for some time, you should consult the vet. You may also want him to check the mother about two weeks before the birth to make sure that everything is going ahead normally.

After the kittens are born you can change the bedding, and make sure that all the kittens are suckling properly. Consult the vet if there are any problems. Keep handling to a minimum. Don't let a tom near the kittens.

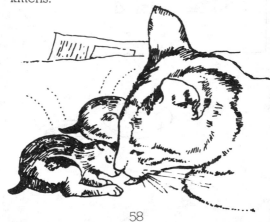

Kittens

A normal litter will consist of three or four kittens. These will be born about every half hour. When they are born they will be blind, and their eyes will remain shut for up to ten days.

Normally the kittens settle down quite happily to feed. Sometimes a kitten may be pushed away from a nipple and will cry. This is quite all right, provided it doesn't happen frequently to the same kitten. If it does, and the kitten loses weight because of it, it may be possible to hand-rear the kitten. It may be, however, that the kitten has something wrong with it. In this case it may be a kindness to have it put to sleep—ask the vet.

After a few days the mother may decide to move the kittens. She will pick them up in her mouth to do this. Don't try to stop her from doing so, it is quite safe and normal, and they will soon settle down in their new location.

After about three weeks the kittens are ready to be weaned. The first sign is usually that they drink milk from the mother's bowl. When they start to do this you can offer them milk of their own—this can be a proprietary milk for human babies, or a special mix for kittens. Serve luke-warm.

After the first day or so a little baby cereal (a crumbled rusk for example) can be added. After another week, offer a meat based baby food. A week after this you can offer finely chopped meat. Gradually increase the amounts of solids until, by eight weeks, they are eating nothing but solid food.

Your cat

Use this chart to keep the details of your cat handy, and to record any medical treatment.

Name ....

Sex ....Breed ....

Description ....

When born ....When acquired ....

Vet ....

Address ....

Telephone ....

Influenza injection: Date ....

Booster due ....

Enteritis injection: Date ....

Booster due

Operation ....

Operation ....

Feeding, kitten:

Time ....Amount ....

Time ....Amount ....

Time ....Amount ....

Time ....Amount ....

Time ....Amount ....

Cat:

Time ....Amount ....

Time ....Amount ....

Time ....Amount ....

Stick your cat's photograph here